MERCY
The Gift Before and Beyond Faith

by

Dr. Doyle Harrison

and

Dr. Michael Landsman

HARRISON HOUSE
Tulsa, Oklahoma

2nd Printing
Over 10,000 in Print

MERCY—The Gift Before and Beyond Faith
ISBN 0-89274-305-0
Copyright © 1984 by Faith Christian Fellowship
P. O. Box 35443
Tulsa, Oklahoma 74153

Published by Harrison House, Inc.
P. O. Box 35035
Tulsa, Oklahoma 74153

Contents

Introduction   1

1 Mercy Defined   5

2 God's Mercy—Old Testament and
  New   9

3 Faith in God's Mercy   27

4 David's Cry for Mercy   39

5 God's Mercy Endures Forever   45

6 Mercy—Before and Beyond Faith   49

7 Come Boldly and Obtain   57

Conclusion   59

Introduction

Throughout life there are special occasions in which gifts are exchanged. Birthdays, Christmas, anniversaries—all are times for the giving of gifts as expressions of love between relatives and friends.

The most outstanding gift ever given was the Lord Jesus Christ. Almighty God gave His only Son to die for the sins of mankind. Besides the gift of Jesus, the Father God has provided an abundance of gifts and blessings for His people: salvation, the infilling of the Holy Spirit, healing, the gifts of the Spirit, and many more.

As we think on these things, how precious our faith becomes—not just the supernatural gift of faith to receive miracles, but faith itself. God has provided for us, His children, faith to overcome the world—faith to stand in the face of defeat and proclaim victory through the power of Jesus' name.

1

The gifts God has given us are precious treasures in our lives.

Hebrews 4:16 links together four spiritual elements: faith, grace, mercy, and boldness. It reads:

Let us therefore come boldly unto the throne of grace, that we may obtain mercy, and find grace to help in time of need.

Though the word *faith* is not included in this verse, it is the subject of Hebrews 3 and 4. As a preface to verse 16, this entire passage shows how faith gives us the boldness and confidence to approach the throne of God.

By virtue of our position in Christ, we can stand before the throne of God's grace, clothed in God's own righteousness. . . . **Christ Jesus our Lord: in whom we have boldness and access with confidence by the faith of him** (Eph. 3:11,12).

Grace is God's unmerited favor. It has been defined by one individual as God's willingness to use His power on our behalf, even though we do not deserve it.

Volumes of material have been written in recent years about faith, about the grace of God, and about boldness. But little has been presented concerning God's mercy.

The mercy of God is an intriguing subject. It is, we believe, one of the least understood facets of the character of God. Many things have been manifested in our lives clearly as a result, not of faith, but of God's grace and mercy.

Mercy is an attribute of God's nature that often has been discounted and almost scoffed at. Many have viewed it as a panacea or cure-all without really understanding its true depths. Though unsure whether God would move on their behalf, people have held to the belief that if they cried out to Him for mercy, it just might work.

God's mercy is a powerful force that can be used by all believers. As quoted in Hebrews 4:16, we are to come boldly to the throne of grace to ***obtain mercy*** *and find grace to help in time of need.* If mercy

3

were not important, we would not be told to obtain it in time of need.

Mercy is not the antithesis of faith, but rather an expression of God's love requiring us to exercise our faith to produce results for others.

Mercy is the gift *before* and *beyond* faith!

1
Mercy Defined

The mercy of God can best be understood by allowing the Word of God to define it through example and precept. But first let's consider these formal definitions:

Webster's Unabridged Dictionary defines mercy as "kindness in excess of what may be expected or demanded by fairness; a disposition to forgive; forbearance and compassion."

The Greek word for mercy is *eleos*. W. E. Vine's *Expository Dictionary*[1] defines *eleos* as "the outward manifestation of pity (compassion); it assumes need on the part of him who receives it, and resources adequate to meet the need on the part of him who shows it."

---

[1] W. E. Vine, *An Expository Dictionary of New Testament Words* (Old Tappan, New Jersey: Fleming H. Revell Company), Vol. 3, p. 60.

We find mercy linked with grace in many instances. Vine continues: "Mercy is the act of God, peace is the resulting experience in the heart of man. Grace describes God's attitude toward the law-breaker and the rebel; mercy is His attitude toward those who are in distress." When used in the verb form, it means "to feel sympathy with the misery of another." This is manifested in actions that will alleviate the misery.

God's mercy is a multi-faceted aspect of His nature and will for mankind, designed for one purpose: to help those in need.

A simple definition of mercy could be "an outward manifestation of sympathetic sorrow for someone's suffering, distress, or unhappiness." Though it is an outward manifestation of compassion, mercy should not be confused with pity.

Mercy carries many meanings, as we have already seen. But there is a deeper, fuller connotation that we should be aware of.

In his *Devotional Word Studies*[2], Dick Mills brings out the following points while quoting other writers:

> Mercy is ''. . . . . . compassionate to those in trouble, even if their trouble is their own foolish making'' (C. Leslie Mittion).

> ''Thus in Christian thought *eleos* means mercy for the man who is in trouble, even if the trouble is his own fault'' (William Barkley).

> ''The true wisdom, the wisdom which God gives, looks upon men in light of God. It bears with their sins, pities their sorrows, is strenuous in the endeavor to relieve sufferings, and to turn them to the habits of a virtuous, honourable and Christian life'' (R. W. Dale).[3]

It would be appropriate to include Warren Wiersbe's comment on the difference between grace and mercy: ''God's grace gives us what we do not deserve, while God's mercy does not give us what we do deserve.''[4] This can be seen when comparing two Scripture references:

---

[2]Dick Mills, *Devotional Word Studies* (Hemet, California: Dick Mills Ministries), p. 3.

[3]Ibid.

[4]Ibid.

For by grace are ye saved **through faith; and that not of yourselves: it is the gift of God;**

Not of works, lest any man should boast.
Ephesians 2:8,9

But after that the kindness and love of God our Saviour toward man appeared,

Not by works of righteousness which we have done, but *according to his mercy he saved us,* **by the washing of regeneration, and renewing of the Holy Ghost;**

Which he shed on us abundantly through Jesus Christ our Saviour;

That *being justified by his grace,* **we should be made heirs according to the hope of eternal life.**
Titus 3:4-7

By **grace** and **mercy** we are saved and allowed to receive that which we do not deserve and did not earn. We deserved destruction and separation from God, but His mercy stepped in. Mercy would not give us what we deserved, then grace gave us what we did not earn.

Mercy and grace are two cooperative forces. They work together for our benefit in every area of our relationship and fellowship with God.

2
God's Mercy—
Old Testament and New

Throughout the Old and New Testaments, God's overwhelming desire was to deal with His people by virtue of mercy. In the Old Testament we see this displayed in the design of the tabernacle.

. . . as Moses was admonished of God when he was about to make the tabernacle: for, See, saith he, that thou make all things according to the pattern shewed to thee in the mount.

Hebrews 8:5

The tabernacle which Moses constructed was a duplication of that which he was shown by God. It was a picture of the true tabernacle in the heavenlies and a shadow of things to come. Moses faithfully complied with God's instructions. (See Ex. 25-27.) According to this pattern, certain elements had to be constructed.

The Ark of the Covenant was made of wood and overlaid in gold. Within the Ark were placed the tables of stone (The Ten Commandments), an omer of manna, and Aaron's rod that budded.

Within the tabernacle were the table for the shewbread and other instruments. In intrinsic value the two most valuable elements were the candlestick and the mercy seat. Their intrinsic value can be used as a measure of their spiritual importance.

The seven-bowled candlestick is representative of the Holy Spirit or the fullness of the Spirit. This can be seen in Revelation, chapter 1. The seven spirits of God mentioned here are not seven different spirits, but seven distinct manifestations of the Spirit of God. Like the candlestick—one instrument with seven vessels for light which drew oil from the whole—so it is with the Spirit of God. He is one Spirit with different manifestations.

The candlestick, made of solid beaten gold, held a place of honor in the tabernacle. But it was the mercy seat which held preeminence, even above the candlestick. It was above all elements within the tabernacle.

The mercy seat was the ever-living witness before the presence of God of the atonement for the people's sins and His determination to deal with them by virtue of mercy. When the blood of an animal was sprinkled upon the mercy seat, God looked down upon that blood and judged by means of mercy.

The mercy seat, also made of pure gold, was constructed to the dimensions of the Ark and served as its covering. The design of the mercy seat included two gold cherubims, one at either end with their wings outstretched to cover it. In his book, *Gleanings In Exodus*, Arthur W. Pink states: ''The Mercy Seat, according to its intrinsic worth, was the most valuable of all the holy vessels.''[1]

We can see the value of the mercy seat by examining some New Testament writ-

---

[1]Arthur W. Pink, *Gleanings In Exodus* (Chicago: Moody Press, 1981) p. 201.

ings. For instance, in Romans 3:25 we read of Jesus Christ:

Whom God hath set forth to be a *propitiation* through faith in his blood, to declare his righteousness for the remission of sins that are past, through the forbearance of God.

The Greek word translated *propitiation* in this verse is the same word used in Hebrews 9:5 to describe the mercy seat. Arthur Pink states: ''It were better . . . if we rendered Kapporeth (the Hebrew word) by *propitiatory* rather than *mercy seat* . . . .''[2]

Jesus thus becomes our propitiatory—the place where the abiding value of the sacrifice stood as a witness before God. Jesus is the ever-living witness of our justification and of the appeasement of God's wrath toward us.

The mercy seat was to stand as a constant reminder to mankind of God's provision for our justification, and to God of His mercy and forgiveness to His people. In essence, the mercy seat was

---

[2]Ibid.

God's throne here on earth. A throne is the place a king sits to execute his authority and where the people come to meet with him. It is at the throne that a king's presence is both seen and felt.

A careful study of the Scriptures will reveal that God's plan and purpose has always been to deal with His people by mercy, notjudgment. The mercy of God overshadowed and overrode the Mosaic Law with its strict code of dos and don'ts. The Law exposed the need in man, but God's mercy went beyond the Law. A law is only meant to expose the transgression of those who break it. Mercy not only takes care of the offense, it pardons the transgressor.

In the minds of some individuals the Ark of the Covenant was the most important element in Israel because it held The Ten Commandments. But God did not make His presence known to the people from the Ark. He made His presence known from the mercy seat.

And thou shalt put the mercy seat above upon the ark; and in the ark thou shalt put the testimony that I shall give thee.

13

And *there I will meet with thee, and I will commune with thee from above the mercy seat,* from between the two cherubims which are upon the ark of the testimony, of all things which I will give thee in commandment unto the children of Israel.

Exodus 25:21,22

And when Moses was gone into the tabernacle . . . to speak with him (God), then he heard the voice of one speaking unto him from off the mercy seat . . . and he spake unto him.

Numbers 7:89

And the Lord said unto Moses . . . I will appear in the cloud upon the mercy seat.

Leviticus 16:2

These and other scriptures indicate that God dwells in mercy. (See 1 Sam. 4:4; 2 Sam. 6:2; 2 Kings 19:15; Ps. 80:1; 99:1.)

The Lord was saying to Moses (and to us), ''When I commune with you, I will do it from the mercy seat.'' Jesus, of course, is our mercy seat, so the pattern of mercy was a foreshadow of Jesus' ministry to the Church.

Blood of Atonement

The Old Testament sacrificial system for the Day of Atonement was unique and sometimes misunderstood. It is outlined in Leviticus 16:3-22.

Two goats were used in the atonement ceremony. One goat, a clean lamb, was killed and its blood placed upon the mercy seat. It was this blood, untainted by sin, which was used to make an atonement for the sins of the nation. The second goat was the scapegoat upon which the sins of the nation were laid. This scapegoat was led outside the camp into the wilderness and let go, thus taking the sins of the people away from the nation.

Only the high priest was allowed to enter into the Holy of Holies, and then only once a year. He took the lamb's blood into the Holy of Holies to make atonement for the sins of the people, including himself.

The high priestly garments are described in Exodus 39. It is especially interesting to note that around the hem of his garment hung alternately pomegranates and bells. Their clanging sound let the people outside know that the high priest was still alive as he performed his yearly duty behind the veil.

And they made upon the hems of the robe pomegranates of blue, and purple, and scarlet, and twined linen.

And they made bells of pure gold, and put the bells between the pomegranates upon the hem of the robe, round about between the pomegranates;

A bell and a pomegranate, a bell and a pomegranate, round about the hem of the robe to minister in; as the Lord commanded Moses.
Exodus 39:24-26

In Hebrews 9:1-5 we see that Jesus is the One Who has taken the blood of the spotless Lamb—His own blood—into the heavenly Holy of Holies. But as mentioned earlier, Jesus is not only the High Priest, He is the mercy seat. (Heb. 9:5; Rom. 3:25.) Jesus is the ever-living Witness before God of His mercy toward us.

Living Witnesses of God's Mercy

As the Old Testament high priest emerged from the Holy of Holies, he stood as a symbol to the people of God's mercy toward them. The very fact of his being alive signified that God had accepted their sacrifice. He then became the ever-living witness before them of the mercy of God. Every time they saw him, they could remember that God was dealing with them by His mercy.

In the same way believers today stand as living witnesses to the world of God's mercy. When people look at Christians, they are seeing a living demonstration of God's mercy. God has not given us what we deserve and has given us what we do not deserve.

Now thanks be unto God, which always causeth us to triumph in Christ, and maketh manifest the savour of his knowledge by us in every place.

For we are unto God a sweet savour of Christ, in them that are saved, and in them that perish:

To the one we are the savour of death unto death; and to the other the savour of life unto life. And who is sufficient for these things?
2 Corinthians 2:14-16

We are the manifest "savour of his knowledge to the world." Unto God we are a sweet savour of Christ. To the world we are the savour of death.

In whom also ye are circumcised with the circumcision made without hands, in putting off the body of the sins of the flesh by the circumcision of Christ:

Buried with him in baptism, wherein also ye are risen with him through the faith of the operation of God, who hath raised him from the dead.

And you, being dead in your sins and the uncircumcision of your flesh, hath he quickened together with him, having forgiven you all trespasses;

Blotting out the handwriting of ordinances that was against us, which was contrary to us, and took it out of the way, nailing it to his cross;

And having spoiled principalities and powers, he made a shew of them openly, triumphing over them in it.

Colossians 2:11-15

I am crucified with Christ: nevertheless I live; yet not I, but Christ liveth in me: and the life which I now live in the flesh I live by the faith of the Son of God, who loved me, and gave himself for me.

Galatians 2:20

We are examples to the world of both death and life: death to the things of the world, life to the things of God. We have been taken out of the control of the dominion of darkness and have been translated into the Kingdom of God.

God has always given to the world a living witness of Himself. It is therefore not strange to view ourselves as living witnesses of God's mercy. In Acts 1:8, Jesus told His followers that when the Holy Spirit came upon them, they would be witnesses. On the day of Pentecost, they became witnesses of the power of God when they were filled with the Holy Spirit and began to speak with other tongues as the Spirit gave them utterance. (Acts 2:2-4.)

We believers are living witnesses of God's mercy, for all that God is and does stems from love, and mercy is one of the primary by-products of love.

God's Mercy vs. Religion

The Pharisaical Jews could not understand how God would deal with His people by mercy and not judgment. They wanted to be dealt with by law, so the

Mosaic Law was set down. God provided for them a complete set of rules and regulations that they could follow.

In time, they became totally wrapped up in the Law. As a result, they forgot the principle of God's mercy, even though God constantly reminded them of it. The tabernacle itself included a reminder: God dealt with them from above the *mercy seat.*

The prophet Micah addressed the religious leaders of his day, as well as the nation of Israel, when he said: **He hath shewed thee, O man, what is good; and what doth the Lord require of thee, but to do justly, and to *love mercy*, and to walk humbly with thy God?** (Mic. 6:8). These people had become so involved with their laws that they had forgotten justice, mercy, and their walk with the Lord.

Jesus rebuked the religious leaders of His day for placing their traditions above the Word of God. He said that their traditions made the Word of God ineffective and that their worship was vain because they had left the Word for tradition. (Mark 7:6-13.)

In Matthew's Gospel, Jesus proclaimed:

But go ye and learn what that meaneth, I will have mercy, and not sacrifice: for I am not come to call the righteous, but sinners to repentance.
Matthew 9:13

But if ye had known what this meaneth, I will have mercy, and not sacrifice, ye would not have condemned the guiltless.

Matthew 12:7

In these scriptures Jesus was referring to Hosea 6:6 which reads: *For I desired mercy, and not sacrifice; and the knowledge of God more than burnt offerings.*

God's fervent desire is to deal with His people through mercy rather than judgment. Judgment will come if one does not avail himself of mercy, but God's mercy is *from everlasting to everlasting upon them that fear* (reverence) *him* (Ps. 103:17).

Mercy and Compassion

Another aspect of God's mercy is His **compassion.** Throughout the four

Gospels Jesus is described as having been
moved with or by compassion.

Webster defines compassion as ''a
suffering with another; hence, sympathy;
sorrow for the distress or misfortunes of
another, with the desire to help.'' Vine's
Expository Dictionary says it means ''to be
moved as to one's inwards.''[3] Compassion flows from the seat of the emotions
and is a strong, compelling desire to help
someone in distress.

Though compassion is a tremendous
moving force, it is useless without mercy.
Compassion lies within the heart; mercy
is the outward manifestation of that
which is felt in the heart. Compassion
feels the need; mercy *fills* the need. Let's
use an illustration.

Suppose a friend who is in desperate
need of a hundred dollars comes to you
and asks for a loan. Your heart goes out
to him and you sincerely desire to help;
but at that particular time you lack the

[3]Vine, Vol. 1, p. 218.

money. Though you have compassion, you cannot show mercy.

A number of years ago when I would see people whose bodies were crippled or full of disease, I had compassion in my heart toward them, but I was not able to help. I would think how Satan had robbed them and would feel the agony they were going through. Inwardly I would ache and hurt for them. Though I had compassion, I had nothing to give them.

Thank God, now I not only have the compassion, I have something tangible to give them: the healing and miracle-working power of God. Not only do I have compassion, I am able to have mercy as well. I have the goods to meet their needs, and compassion compels me to them.

To meet a person's need, both mercy and compassion must be in operation. Compassion compels us to the one in need; mercy meets the need.

Here is a Biblical example of both compassion and mercy in operation through the ministry of the Lord Jesus:

And as they departed from Jericho, a great multitude followed him.

And, behold, two blind men sitting by the way side, when they heard that Jesus passed by, cried out, saying, Have mercy on us, O Lord, thou Son of David.

And the multitude rebuked them, because they should hold their peace: but they cried the more, saying, Have mercy on us, O Lord, thou Son of David.

And Jesus stood still, and called them, and said, What will ye that I shall do unto you?

They say unto him, Lord, that our eyes may be opened. So *Jesus had compassion on them, and touched their eyes:* and immediately their eyes received sight, and they followed him.

Matthew 20:29-34

These two who were crying out for mercy addressed Jesus as the Son of David. This shows that they recognized authority. They knew that Jesus not only had the means to meet their need, but the authority as well. (You will be unable to do anything with faith unless you understand authority.)

When Jesus heard their cry, the compassion of God within Him rose up and dictated His actions. He stopped and called for them to be brought to Him. Then when he touched their eyes, immediately they received sight.

This action was mercy in operation. Those two men had faith that God through Jesus would be merciful to them. Their faith was in God's mercy, and Jesus responded at the point of their faith.

3
Faith in God's Mercy

Another person who reached out to Jesus with faith in God's mercy was a Canaanite woman. We read from Matthew's Gospel:

Then Jesus went thence, and departed into the coasts of Tyre and Sidon.

And, behold, a woman of Canaan came out of the same coasts, and cried unto him, saying, Have mercy on me, O Lord, thou Son of David; my daughter is grievously vexed with a devil.

But he answered her not a word. And his disciples came and besought him, saying, Send her away; for she crieth after us.

But he answered and said, I am not sent but unto the lost sheep of the house of Israel.

Then came she and worshipped him, saying, Lord, help me.

But he answered and said, It is not meet to take the children's bread, and to cast it to dogs.

And she said, Truth, Lord: yet the dogs eat of the crumbs which fall from their masters' table.

Then Jesus answered and said unto her, O woman, great is thy faith: be it unto thee even as thou wilt. And her daughter was made whole from that very hour.

Matthew 15:21-28

This incident occurred just after Jesus and His disciples had experienced a confrontation with the scribes and Pharisees. They were questioning why Jesus had allowed His disciples to transgress the traditions of the elders by eating with unwashed hands. (Matt. 15:2.)

The washing to which they referred was not for hygienic purposes; it was a ceremonial washing. According to tradition, after the Jews had completed their hygienic washing, they were to stand over a basin of water and wash to the elbows, then hold their arms in the air, allowing the water to drip from their elbows.

Jesus responded to their criticism by calling them hypocrites and saying, **Why do ye also transgress the commandment**

of God by your tradition? . . . Thus have ye made the commandment of God of none effect by your tradition (Matt. 15:3,6).

These religious men had no concept of God's mercy. To them God was a hard taskmaster who had set down a series of rules, regulations, and traditions that were not to be broken.

After this confrontation, Jesus and His disciples left. In Mark 7:24 we see that they went to the coast to rest. It says they entered a house and did not want anyone to know.

Into this setting came a Gentile woman. To the Jews she was an outcast, an unbeliever. She approached Jesus and cried out, "Have mercy on me, Lord!" Receiving no response from Him, she cried all the more.

The disciples probably were thinking, "How dare she come along and make such a fuss! If she keeps screaming, she'll attract a lot of attention and ruin our vacation!" (Now don't get religious in your thinking. These men were people

29

just like you and me. They took time to get away and rest. They wanted to play, not pray!)

The situation was made even worse when Jesus did not answer her. This woman was crying out for mercy, but Jesus would not respond. The disciples asked the Lord to send her away. In other words, they were saying, "Lord, get rid of her before she attracts too many people. We don't want a scene. If You don't do something, everybody in this area will know You are here and will want to be ministered to." They were so wrapped up in their own desires that they failed to think about the needs of others.

When Jesus did speak, His words were directed to His disciples. He said, "I am not sent, but unto the lost sheep of the house of Israel."

Jesus was seemingly ignoring the need of an individual, treating her as a Gentile, an unclean person who does not rate His time or attention.

The woman must have heard His words to the disciples, but she remained undaunted, determined to receive the results she desired. Refusing to become discouraged, she came to Jesus and worshipped Him. Did she quote Isaiah 53:3-5, or Psalm 103:3, or Exodus 15:26? No! She cried, "Lord, help me!" She knew nothing about the Word of God. There was only one thought in her mind: *I need help, and Jesus can provide that help.* She came to Jesus asking for mercy.

The answer she received from Him does not fit the image we have of Jesus. His words seemed harsh, even cruel, when He said, "It's not right to take bread which has been provided for the children and cast it to the dogs."

Was He adding insult to injury? First He refused to answer her, then He called her a dog.

Jesus was not insulting her by making a statement of her value and self-worth. He was stating a religious fact. As a Gentile, she was not entitled to that which had been provided to the children of Israel. She had no covenant right to healing or deliverance. Jesus' mission was primarily to reach the lost sheep of the house of Israel.

We can see this more clearly by reading Paul's words to the Ephesian church:

Wherefore remember, that ye being in time past Gentiles in the flesh, who are called Uncircumcision by that which is called Circumcision in the flesh made by hands;

That at that time ye were *without Christ, being aliens from the commonwealth of Israel, and strangers from the covenants of promise, having no hope, and without God in the world.*
Ephesians 2:11,12

Jesus was telling this woman that the time of the Gentiles was not yet. As a Gentile, she was an alien from the nation of Israel to whom all the promises had been given, and as such she had no covenant right to receive help.

Her response is the perfect example of an undaunted spirit. She said, *Truth, Lord: yet the dogs eat of the crumbs which fall from the masters' table.* She was, in essence, saying: ''Yes, it's true that I am without Christ. It's true that I am an alien from Israel and a stranger from the covenants of promise. I *am* without God, **but I'm not without hope!** Even the unbeliever has a right to mercy. I don't want the children's bread. I just want mercy!''

She understood a fact which the prophet Joel had written: **Whosoever shall call on the name of the Lord shall be delivered** (Joel 2:32).

Jesus replied by giving her a position not held by any Jew at that time. He said, *O woman, great is thy faith.*

Great Faith

Only two individuals were acknowledged by Jesus as having great faith, and both were Gentiles. Besides this Canaanite woman, there was a Roman centurion. We read his story in Matthew, chapter 8:

And when Jesus was entered into Capernaum, there came unto him a centurion, beseeching him, and saying, Lord, my servant lieth at home sick of the palsy, grievously tormented.

And Jesus saith unto him, I will come and heal him.

The centurion answered and said, Lord, I am not worthy that thou shouldest come under my roof: but speak the word only, and my servant shall be healed.

Matthew 8:5-8

This man was not trying to be humble; he was stating religious fact. As a Gentile he was not worthy for a Jew to come into his house. By Jewish standards he was a dog, like the Canaanite woman. He continued:

For I am a man under authority, having soldiers under me: and I say to this man, Go, and he goeth; and to another, Come, and he cometh; and to my servant, Do this, and he doeth it.

When Jesus heard it, he marvelled, and said to them that followed, Verily I say unto you, I have not found so great faith, no, not in Israel.

And Jesus said unto the centurion, Go thy way; and as thou hast believed, so be it done unto thee. And his servant was healed in the selfsame hour.

Matthew 8:9,10,13

Exercising Faith for Others

Both these Gentiles came to the Lord, cried out to Him, received from Him, and were said to have great faith.

The Canaanite woman was an outcast, but her faith in God's mercy took her beyond the religious traditions of that day. The Roman centurion, recognizing authority, placed his faith in the authority in which Jesus walked.

What made these two individuals so different from all the others who reached out to Jesus? Both were concerned with the plight of another person. The Canaanite woman sought deliverance for her daughter; the Roman centurion sought healing for his servant.

Great faith is not believing in your heart and confessing with your mouth. (That is the God kind of faith. See Mark 11:23.)

Great faith is not having your own personal needs met.

Great faith is exercising your faith on behalf of another person—using your faith to meet the needs of another.

Remember Mercy

Some individuals have accepted "the faith message," but developed a hard attitude, especially regarding healing. To them it is: Believe God or die!

Unfortunately this is often how the faith message is portrayed. It is true that without faith it is impossible to please God and that the just shall live by faith. But we must not become like the Pharisees. We must remember mercy.

How many times have we become so religious in our walk of faith that we have failed to show mercy? How often have we separated ourselves and others from the mercy of God?

God has given us the measure of faith, but that does not give us the right to look down our noses at those who may be weak in faith. Romans 14:1 says, **Him that is weak in the faith receive ye, but not to doubtful disputations.** If a person is weak in faith, we are to receive him without judging his doubtful thoughts.

How many times have we turned people away because they did not meet our "faith specifications"? How often have we looked at our brothers and sisters in the Lord and said, with just a touch of superiority in our voices, "They failed to receive because they didn't have enough faith"?

John G. Lake overheard one of his workers turning away an individual from a healing service. The worker asked if the person had faith to be healed. When the person responded that he did not, the worker said he would be unable to receive healing because he had no faith. Upon hearing this conversation, Dr. Lake rebuked his worker and instructed him never to turn away a person for lack of faith. In Dr. Lake's view, they could get the individual healed on their faith, then teach him faith.

This is an attitude all Christians should develop. Always remember that it is God's will to meet the needs of the people. Whether through our faith, their faith, the gifts of the Spirit, or His mercy, God will reach the people on their level.

Let us not forget mercy. We have the spiritual weapons at our disposal to keep the enemy in retreat. But should our faith seem impaired, we can cry out for the mercy of God. His mercy helps us enter into faith's rest. We realize that even when our aim is off target, God in His mercy will meet our needs anyway.

God's mercy existed *before* our faith, and it will extend *beyond* our faith.

4

David's Cry for Mercy

David understood the mercy of God. In a desperate time of need in his own life, he cried out for mercy and it was granted him.

In the Second Book of Samuel, chapters 11 and 12, we see David transgressing against the law of the Lord by committing adultery with Bathsheba. When she became pregnant, David added to his sin by ordering that her husband, Uriah, a devoted soldier, be killed in battle. This was premeditated murder.

Once Uriah was dead and Bathsheba's time of mourning was over, she became David's wife and bore him a son. **But the thing that David had done displeased the Lord** (2 Sam. 11:27).

Under the Old Covenant there were two basic types of disobedience: sin and transgression.

Sin meant to miss the mark, carrying the connotation as of an archer who shoots at a target but misses. Because the person was attempting to do the right thing, but fell short, a sacrifice for sin was allowed so that fellowship with the Lord could be restored.

Transgression was another matter. The Hebrew word for transgression meant a revolt, a rebellion, or to apostatize. Even though a person knows the way the Lord wants him to go, he willfully turns his back and goes his own way. Under the Law there was no sacrifice or forgiveness for the transgressor. He was to be put to death. The transgressor was worse than an infidel and was doomed for eternity. This is the position in which David had placed himself.

The prophet Nathan comes to David and confronts him with a parable:

There were two men in one city; the one rich, and the other poor.

The rich man had exceeding many flocks and herds:

But the poor man had nothing, save one little ewe lamb, which he had bought and nourished up: and it grew up together with him, and with his children; it did eat of his own meat, and drank of his own cup, and lay in his bosom, and was unto him as a daughter.

And there came a traveller unto the rich man, and he spared to take of his own flock and of his own herd, to dress for the wayfaring man that was come unto him; but took the poor man's lamb, and dressed it for the man that was come to him.

2 Samuel 12:1-4

David reacted in anger to this parable, saying to Nathan, *As the Lord liveth, the man that hath done this thing shall surely die* (v. 5).

Nathan responded, **Thou art the man** (v. 7). David admitted his sin, then cried out to God for mercy. His plea is recorded in Psalm 51:

Have mercy upon me, O God, according to thy lovingkindness: according unto the multitude of thy tender mercies blot out my transgressions.

Wash me throughly from mine iniquity, and cleanse me from my sin.

For I acknowledge my transgressions: and my sin is ever before me.

Against thee, thee only, have I sinned, and done this evil in thy sight: that thou mightest be justified when thou speakest, and be clear when thou judgest (vv. 1-4).

Such a request was unheard of in Israel. Everyone knew there was no forgiveness for transgression under the Law. But David did not attempt to approach God on the basis of the Law; he cried out for mercy.

Notice David's attitude. He recognized his transgression and immediately cried out for the Lord to pardon him according to mercy. He wanted God to do more than merely cover over his transgressions. He wanted Him, by virtue of the multitude of His tender mercies, to blot out his transgressions. He said:

Purge me with hyssop, and I shall be clean: wash me, and I shall be whiter than snow.

Hide thy face from my sins, and blot out all mine iniquities.

Create in me a clean heart, O God; and renew a right spirit within me.

Cast me not away from thy presence; and take not thy holy spirit from me.

42

Restore unto me the joy of thy salvation; and uphold me with thy free spirit.

Psalm 51:7,9-12

All the things David asked for were fulfilled in Christ. Let's read Colossians 2:13-15.

And you, being dead in your sins and the uncircumcision of your flesh, hath he quickened together with him, having forgiven you all *trespasses;*

Blotting out the handwriting of ordinances that was against us, which was contrary to us, and took it out of the way, nailing it to his cross;

And having spoiled principalities and powers, he made a shew of them openly, triumphing over them in it.

David, by faith in God's mercy, reached out for that which was to come through the blood of Jesus. He carried it even farther when he said:

For thou desirest not sacrifice; else would I give it: thou delightest not in burnt offering.

The sacrifices of God are a broken spirit: a broken and a contrite heart, O God, thou wilt not despise.

Psalm 51:16,17

David had realized that the Law was only a guideline to show men how to live and that God desired to deal with His people by virtue of His mercy.

It was God's mercy at work when the prophet Nathan said to David, **The Lord also hath put away thy sin; thou shalt not die** (2 Sam. 12:13). David's transgression was forgiven because he was quick to repent and call upon God's mercy.

David's life provides clear evidence that God's mercy endures forever.

5

God's Mercy
Endures Forever

God has always desired to deal with His people in lovingkindness and mercy. Psalm 136 shows how eternal God's mercy is. Over and over, it reminds us of this one fact: **God's mercy endureth forever.**

Let's look at the entire psalm.

O give thanks unto the Lord; for he is good: for his mercy endureth for ever.

O give thanks unto the God of gods: for his mercy endureth for ever.

To him who alone doeth great wonders: for his mercy endureth for ever.

To him that by wisdom made the heavens: for his mercy endureth for ever.

To him that stretched out the earth above the waters: for his mercy endureth for ever.

To him that made great lights: for his mercy endureth for ever:

The sun to rule by day: for his mercy endureth for ever:

The moon and stars to rule by night: for his mercy endureth for ever.

To him that smote Egypt in their firstborn: for his mercy endureth for ever:

And brought out Israel from among them: for his mercy endureth for ever:

With a strong hand, and with a stretched out arm: for his mercy endureth for ever.

To him who divided the Red Sea into parts: for his mercy endureth for ever.

And made Israel pass through the midst of it: for his mercy endureth for ever:

But overthrew Pharaoh and his host in the Red Sea: for his mercy endureth for ever.

To him who led his people through the wilderness: for his mercy endureth for ever.

To him which smote great kings: for his mercy endureth for ever.

And slew famous kings: for his mercy endureth for ever.

And Og the king of Bashan: for his mercy endureth for ever.

And gave their land for an heritage: for his mercy endureth for ever.

Even an heritage unto Israel his servant: for his mercy endureth for ever.

And hath redeemed us from our enemies: for his mercy endureth for ever.

Who giveth food to all flesh: for his mercy endureth for ever.

O give thanks unto the God of heaven: for his mercy endureth for ever.

Notice that there is a colon in each verse, separating the first statement from the second. A colon indicates two separate thoughts joined together for a point of emphasis. Each thought is independent and can stand alone; but for the sake of emphasis, they are joined. The two thoughts are linked together for a specific purpose: to display a contrast.

The Psalmist David by inspiration of the Holy Spirit is highlighting certain events: the death of the firstborn in Egypt, the creation of the heavens and the earth, the dividing of the Red Sea, the death of great kings, and Israel receiving other lands for a heritage.

In contrast to these one-time actions, God's mercy endures forever. The message of Psalm 136 is simple: God's mercy is everlasting and can be depended upon, even when all else fails.

6

Mercy—Before and Beyond Faith

Mercy is a gift which existed long before your faith. It was God's mercy that received you when you were still a sinner. Before you had faith to be saved, God had mercy on you.

Thank God for faith. Thank God that He placed within every believer the measure of faith and gave us His precious Holy Spirit to nurture that faith until it grows and matures within us. But without mercy we would never have been able to receive that measure of faith.

Mercy, which existed long *before* your faith, will exist long *beyond* your faith. It will be in operation when your faith has been extended to its limits. God's mercy is everlasting. It never ends. The mercy of God endureth forever!

If you will settle your faith in the mercy of God, you will enjoy the fullness of His blessings.

Mercy—The Pattern

The mercy of God is a pattern that has been consistent throughout the Word of God. God has always dealt with His people in mercy.

The mercy of God can take various forms. In Psalm 145:8-10 we read:

The Lord is gracious, and full of compassion; slow to anger, and of great mercy.

The Lord is good to all: and his tender mercies are over all his works.

All thy works shall praise thee, O Lord; and thy saints shall bless thee.

This scripture tells us that God's mercy is great, He is good to all, and His tender mercies are over all His works. This means His mercy is the highest motivating factor in His nature. Mercy is the zenith, the apogee, the height of the motivating factors of God. All that God is can be seen in His mercy.

In Ephesians 2:4,5 we read:

But God, who is rich in mercy, for his great love wherewith he loved us,

Even when we were dead in sins, hath quickened us together with Christ, (by grace ye are saved;).

God is rich in mercy. That means He has a full supply and will never run out. His mercies are fresh every morning.

It is of the Lord's mercies that we are not consumed, because his compassions fail not.

They are new every morning: great is thy faithfulness.

Lamentations 3:22,23

Mercy is the pattern whereby God deals with us, and we are to deal with others.

Howbeit for this cause I obtained mercy, **that in me first Jesus Christ might shew forth all longsuffering,** *for a pattern to them which should hereafter believe on him to life everlasting.*

1 Timothy 1:16

If you will read only the underlined portion of the above scripture, you will see that the Apostle Paul is saying he obtained mercy as a pattern for all those who would come to the Lord.

He is stating that if God could deal with him in mercy, it would not be a problem for God to deal with anyone else in mercy.

The Amplified Bible[1] sheds more light on Ephesians 2:4. It reads: ''But God! So rich is He in His mercy! Because of and in order to satisfy the great and wonderful and intense love with which He loved us . . . .''

Once we realize that God is rich in mercy and that His mercy is for our use, we can walk boldly into any situation and know we will be victorious. God's mercy will make up for any deficiencies we may have. **Therefore seeing we have this ministry, as we have received mercy, we faint not** (2 Cor. 4:1). In other words our understanding of mercy will enable us to stand and not give up.

This leads us to understand that because God deals with us by mercy, we should deal with others in mercy.

---

[1]*The Amplified Bible: New Testament* (La Habra, California: The Lockman Foundation, 1954, 1958).

God, our Father, the Most High God, is rich in mercy because of and to satisfy His burning desire to love. He possesses a consuming love, referred to in many verses of Scripture as compassion. He wants to reach out to the world and show mercy toward them.

Blessed are the merciful: for they shall obtain mercy.

Matthew 5:7

Remember, mercy is the outward expression of God's compassion.

In Ephesians 5 we are told to be imitators of God. God operates in mercy. He is plenteous in mercy.

For thou, Lord, art good, and ready to forgive; and plenteous in mercy unto all them that call upon thee.

Psalm 86:5

As imitators of God, we are under obligation to operate in mercy, even toward those who are in problems of their own making.

A good example is Romans 14:1, **Him that is weak in the faith receive ye, but not to doubtful disputations.** The marginal rendering of this is ". . . not to judge his doubtful thoughts." This is mercy in operation.

God is full of mercy, and so are we. It is imperative that we become witnesses to the world of His mercy. When the world sees the mercy of God abounding in us, they will know that God is alive and ready to offer them the forgiveness they need.

Mercy and Kindness

Through mercy, God is able to show His love and kindness toward His people. Again, we quote from Ephesians, chapter 2:

Even when we were dead in sins, (God) hath quickened us together with Christ. . .

And hath raised us up together, and made us sit together in heavenly places in Christ Jesus:

That in the ages to come he might shew the exceeding riches of his grace in his kindness toward us through Christ Jesus (vv. 5-7).

While we were still walking in sin, God brought us to Himself through Christ. We have a place in heaven on the same spiritual level as the Lord Jesus. Why? Because of His love. He wants to display to us the exceeding riches of His grace in His kindness toward us.

A part of God's nature is kindness. Isaiah 54:8 says, **. . . with everlasting kindness will I have mercy on thee, saith the Lord thy Redeemer.**

God's kindness, like His mercy, is everlasting. The two are linked together. He will never fail to be kind; He will never fail to be merciful. Remember one of the definitions of mercy: "kindness in excess of what may be demanded by fairness or expected."

As God's people we need to allow His mercy and kindness to flow through us toward others. This is how we are to be living. We should be kind to one another, tenderhearted, forgiving one another, always demonstrating mercy and kindness to one another.

So much has been taught in recent years about the confession of our mouths—that we are to watch what we say and be sure to speak the right words. But just as we are to watch our confession, we should be as diligent to watch our actions toward others. We are to live by faith, but mercy goes beyond faith. It walks the second mile and turns the other cheek without a begrudging attitude.

Jesus ministered the grace, mercy, and kindness of God in His every action. As Christians we are united with Christ. We are extensions of His compassion and His mercy—partakers of His love and kindness. All that He is has been placed within us. So we must allow it to flow through us to the world.

7

Come Boldly and Obtain

For we have not an high priest which cannot be touched with the feeling of our infirmities; but was in all points tempted like as we are, yet without sin.

Let us therefore come boldly unto the throne of grace, that we may obtain mercy, and find grace to help in time of need.

Hebrews 4:15,16

Jesus Christ, our High Priest, is touched with the feeling of our infirmities. He knows what it is like to be tempted with sin; He has experienced it.

He knows our lack and our need, so He has issued an invitation: Come boldly to the throne of grace that you may obtain mercy and find grace to help in your time of need.

One Scripture verse which ties directly into this passage is Psalm 25:10. It reads:

All the paths of the Lord are mercy and truth unto such as keep his covenant and his testimonies.

All the paths of the Lord are mercy. God is mercy, and His mercy endures forever. It is bottomless, limitless, unending, ever present to His people.

As a child of Almighty God, you can come before Him boldly at any time and obtain mercy to meet your need. So rest in that assurance.

Conclusion

Our intention with this book has been to present a wider view of God's mercy as seen in His Word. Mercy is a vital element in our walk of faith. As an attribute of God, it should be an attribute of every believer.

When mercy is at work within you, you will be willing to take any action necessary within the limits of God's Word to meet the need of another.

God's mercy was in operation before you received salvation and it will be in operation throughout the ages. It will enable you to go beyond your faith in meeting the needs of others. It will undergird your faith and add an element of confidence: you can be assured that when your faith is expended, mercy is always there. It is **the gift before and beyond faith!**

Other Books by Doyle Harrison

Understanding Authority For Effective Leadership

Count It All Joy
Eight Principles To Use For Victory In Times Of
Temptations, Tests, & Trials

Coauthored by Van Gale

Other Books by Michael Landsman

Supportive Ministries

Doubling Your Ability Through God

To obtain these books
you may write:

HARRISON HOUSE
P. O. Box 35035 • Tulsa, OK 74153

or call toll free:
1-800-331-3334